SUNDAY'S FUN DAY, CHARLIE BROWN

PEANUTS CLASSICS

Dr. Beagle and Mr. Hyde
Fly, You Stupid Kite, Fly!
How Long, Great Pumpkin, How Long?
It's Great to Be a Superstar
Kiss Her, You Blockhead!
My Anxieties Have Anxieties
Speak Softly, and Carry a Beagle
There Goes the Shutout
Summers Fly, Winters Walk
Thank Goodness for People
The Beagle Has Landed
What Makes You Think You're Happy?
And a Woodstock in a Birch Tree
A Smile Makes a Lousy Umbrella
The Mad Punter Strikes Again
There's a Vulture Outside
Here Comes the April Fool!
What Makes Musicians So Sarcastic?
A Kiss on the Nose Turns Anger Aside
It's Hard Work Being Bitter
I'm Not Your Sweet Babboo!
Stop Snowing on My Secretary
Always Stick Up for the Underbird
What's Wrong with Being Crabby?
Don't Hassle Me with Your Sighs, Chuck
The Way of the Fussbudget Is Not Easy
You're Weird, Sir!
It's a Long Way to Tipperary
Who's the Funny-Looking Kid with the Big Nose?
Sunday's Fun Day, Charlie Brown
You're Out of Your Mind, Charlie Brown!
You're the Guest of Honor, Charlie Brown

SUNDAY'S FUN DAY, CHARLIE BROWN

by Charles M. Schulz

An Owl Book
Henry Holt and Company/ New York

Henry Holt and Company, Inc.
Publishers since 1866
115 West 18th Street
New York, New York 10011

Henry Holt® is a registered trademark
of Henry Holt and Company, Inc.

Library of Congress Catalog Card Number: 93-79247

ISBN 0-8050-2891-9

Henry Holt books are available for special
promotions and premiums. For details contact:
Director, Special Markets.

Originally published as *Sunday's Fun Day, Charlie
Brown* in 1965 by Holt, Rinehart and Winston.
Published by Holt, Rinehart and Winston in two parts
in two expanded editions under the titles *What's Wrong
with Being Crabby?* in 1976 and *There's a
Vulture Outside* in 1976.

New Owl Book Edition—1993

Printed in the United States of America
All first editions are printed on acid-free paper.∞

1 3 5 7 9 10 8 6 4 2

DO YOU BELIEVE IN PSYCHIC PHENOMENA?

WHY?

I WAS SITTING HERE WATCHING TV WHEN ALL OF A SUDDEN, I FELT A PIECE OF JELLY BREAD CALLING ME!

WHAT'S THE MATTER, SALLY? WHAT HAPPENED? WHY ARE YOU CRYING?

WAAH!

I DON'T KNOW...

I WAS JUMPING ROPE.... EVERYTHING WAS ALL RIGHT... WHEN... I DON'T KNOW...

SUDDENLY IT ALL SEEMED SO FUTILE!

I FEEL OLD-FASHIONED!

AH! A PERFECT DAY!

ALL RIGHT, RISE AN' SHINE! IT'S RABBIT-CHASING TIME!!

OH, GOOD GRIEF!

THE SNOW IS FRESH AND THE AIR IS CLEAR...I PREDICT WE'LL SEE LOTS OF GAME!

HOW CAN YOU CHASE RABBITS IN THE MIDDLE OF THE NIGHT?

WE'LL START HERE...THIS IS A BIG FIELD, AND YOU SHOULD BE ABLE TO PICK UP THE SCENT WITHOUT...

WAKE UP!

OKAY! HERE WE GO!!

SNIF SNIF SNIF SNIF

SNIF SNIF SNIF SNIF SNIF

I GUESS WE'RE NOT GOING TO FIND ANY, SNOOPY, BUT AT LEAST WE TRIED...

EVEN THOUGH YOU'VE FAILED, IT ALWAYS MAKES YOU FEEL BETTER WHEN YOU KNOW YOU'VE DONE YOUR BEST!

I'D HATE TO DISILLUSION HER, BUT I DON'T EVEN KNOW WHAT A RABBIT SMELLS LIKE!

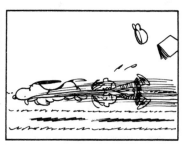

CLOMP!

WHY WAS I LATE FOR SCHOOL TODAY? WELL, IT WAS THIS WAY..

STUPID LEAVES!

A SLIVER!

AAUGH! I GOT A SLIVER!

I GOT A SLIVER IN MY FINGER!

LET'S SEE...

DON'T TOUCH IT! DON'T TOUCH IT!

I'D BETTER GO GET A PAIR OF TWEEZERS...

NO! NO! IT'LL HURT! YOU'LL KILL ME! YOU'LL KILL ME!!

LOOK...YOU WANT TO GET THE SLIVER OUT, DON'T YOU? WELL, HOLD STILL!

WAIT A MINUTE...DIDN'T WE FORGET SOMETHING?

WHILE YOU'RE OPERATING, I THOUGHT I WAS SUPPOSED TO BE BITING ON A BULLET...

HAVE YOU EVER DONE ANY SOAP CARVING?

SOAP CARVING?

YES, IT'S GREAT!

I'VE BEEN WORKING ON THIS MODEL OF AN OLD SAILING VESSEL

I WANT YOU TO SEE IT, CHARLIE BROWN...I CARVED IT ALL BY MYSELF..

I'M ESPECIALLY PROUD OF THE GOOD JOB I DID ON THE SAILS...IT TOOK ME THREE DAYS TO DO JUST THE SAILS ALONE..

IF YOU'RE GOING TO GET YOUR HANDS REALLY CLEAN, YOU'VE GOT TO WORK UP A GOOD LATHER

LOTS OF SOAP AND HOT WATER..THAT'S WHAT DOES IT!

I HAD PLANNED TO SHOW YOU AN AUTHENTIC REPLICA OF AN AMERICAN CLIPPER SHIP.. WOULD YOU SETTLE FOR A CANOE?

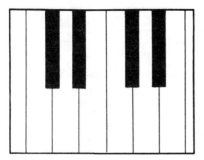

WOW!

LOOK, CHARLIE BROWN! LOOK!

I GOT SOME MONEY FROM THE TOOTH FAIRY!

I PUT A TOOTH UNDER MY PILLOW LAST NIGHT, AND WHEN I WOKE UP THIS MORNING, I FOUND THIS MONEY...

SEE? I GOT A CHECK FOR THIRTY-FIVE CENTS!

A CHECK?!

"PAY TO THE ORDER OF LINUS VAN PELT....THIRTY-FIVE CENTS.. DO NOT FOLD, SPINDLE OR MUTILATE.. KNOW YOUR ENDORSER"

EXPANDED BUSINESS REQUIRES IMPROVED METHODS..

I CAN'T DENY IT!

THIS WAY, LITTLE FRIEND OF MINE..

IT'S GOOD TO HAVE A FRIEND

ALTHOUGH I CAN SEE WHERE HAVING TOO MANY FRIENDS COULD BE HARD ON THE STOMACH!

ORDINARILY, I FROWN ON CARD PLAYING, BUT BRIDGE IS A PRETTY GOOD GAME, AND, AFTER ALL, THEY DO NEED A PLACE TO PLAY...

"PASS"?!

SOME PEOPLE JUST SHOULDN'T PLAY CARDS TOGETHER!

FORTUNATELY, THOSE DOG FOOD COMMERCIALS DON'T COME ON TOO OFTEN!

CALL THE HUMANE SOCIETY FOR ME, AND ASK THEM HOW LONG I'D HAVE TO STAY IN JAIL IF I PUNCHED A BEAGLE IN THE NOSE..

rats!

RATS! I JUST CAN'T DO IT!!

WHAT'S THE MATTER, CHARLIE BROWN?

I CAN'T WRITE LIKE THE TEACHER WANTS US TO..

LOOK AT THIS BOOK...SEE HOW NICE ALL THE LETTERS ARE? I CAN'T WRITE LIKE THAT! I NEVER WILL BE ABLE TO WRITE LIKE THAT!

OF COURSE, YOU CAN'T, CHARLIE BROWN... NEITHER COULD THE PERSON WHO WROTE THIS BOOK...WHAT HE DID, YOU SEE, WAS TAKE THE BEST LETTERS AND MAKE PHOTOSTATS OF THEM

THEN, FROM THESE PHOTOSTATS HE MADE A PASTE-UP OF THE WHOLE PAGE, AND PRINTED IT TO LOOK LIKE IT WAS DONE PERFECTLY..

YOU ARE A VICTIM OF STUDIO TECHNIQUE

WHOM DO I SUE?

STUPID LEAVES!

ONE FINGER WILL MEAN A FAST BALL, TWO FINGERS A CURVE AND THREE FINGERS A SLOW BALL... OKAY?

FINE

WHAT WERE YOU TWO TALKING ABOUT?

WE WERE JUST DISCUSSING OUR SIGNALS

OH..

I THOUGHT MAYBE YOU WERE TALKING ABOUT ME...

I GUESS THAT'S UNDERSTANDABLE IF YOU'RE PARTICULARLY SENSITIVE!

GOLLY! HAVE YOU EVER SEEN SO MANY SNAKES AND LIZARDS IN ALL YOUR LIFE?!! NO... AND SPIDERS, TOO... SPIDERS, TOO? YEAH, SNAKES AND LIZARDS AND SPIDERS!

AND THEY'RE ALL HEADED THIS WAY, YOU SAY? YEAH, THERE'S A WHOLE FLOCK OF 'EM... ALL HEADED THIS WAY... CREEPING AND CRAWLING... SNAKES AN' LIZARDS AN'..

PTUI!

PTUI!

UNTIL IT IS DEMONSTRATED, ONE FORGETS THE REALLY GREAT DIFFERENCE THAT EXISTS BETWEEN THE MERELY COMPETENT AMATEUR AND THE VERY EXPERT PROFESSIONAL

WUMP!

KLUNK

BUMP!

TAKE OFF THOSE STUPID GLASSES!!!

MAKE A GUY A MANAGER, AND RIGHT AWAY HE TURNS INTO A CRABBY OLD MAN!

SCHULZ

IT'S STARTING TO RAIN, CHARLIE BROWN... AREN'T WE GOING TO CALL THE GAME?

NO, WE'RE NOT GOING TO CALL THE GAME, SO YOU MIGHT AS WELL GET BACK OUT THERE IN CENTER FIELD WHERE YOU BELONG!

AND TRY TO PAY ATTENTION TO WHAT YOU'RE DOING!

POW!

BONK

THIS IS GOING TO BE ANOTHER GREAT SEASON!

* SIGH *

THERE'S THAT LITTLE RED-HAIRED GIRL WALKING HOME FROM SCHOOL....JUST THINK... I'M WALKING ON THE SAME SIDEWALK SHE'S WALKING ON

OF COURSE, I'M WALKING SEVEN BLOCKS BEHIND HER, BUT I'M WALKING ON THE VERY SAME SIDEWALK

I WISH I WERE WALKING WITH HER...I WISH I WERE WALKING RIGHT BESIDE HER, AND WE WERE TALKING

SHE WENT INTO THAT NICE HOUSE! SO THAT'S WHERE SHE LIVES...AND THERE'S THE DOOR SHE WENT IN...

I WISH SHE'D INVITE ME OVER TO HER HOUSE SOME TIME.. I WISH SHE'D COME UP TO ME, AND SAY, "WHY DON'T YOU COME OVER TO MY HOUSE AFTER SCHOOL, CHARLIE BROWN?"

THERE SHE IS AGAIN..SHE WENT INTO THE BACK YARD, AND SHE'S SWINGING ON HER SWING-SET...

WE COULD WALK HOME FROM SCHOOL TOGETHER, AND THEN WE COULD SWING ON HER SWING-SET...

BOY, WHAT A BLOCKHEAD I AM! I'LL NEVER GET TO SWING WITH HER! I'LL NEVER GET TO WALK WITH HER! I'LL NEVER EVEN GET TO SAY ONE WORD TO HER!

ALL I GET TO DO IS WALK HOME FROM SCHOOL BY MYSELF, AND....

OH, HI, SNOOPY

YOU'RE NOT MUCH OF A SUBSTITUTE FOR A LITTLE RED-HAIRED GIRL

QUITE OFTEN LATELY I HAVE THE FEELING I DON'T KNOW WHAT'S GOING ON...

SNOOPY, I'D LIKE TO READ YOU A STORY I'VE WRITTEN AND ILLUSTRATED FOR SCHOOL...

"ONCE THERE WAS A LITTLE GIRL WHO HAD A HEADACHE."

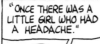

HER MOM GAVE HER SOME PILLS, BUT THEY DIDN'T HELP. HER MOM THEN TOOK HER TO THE DOCTOR.

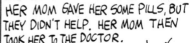

"THE DOCTOR WAS UNABLE TO FIND ANYTHING WRONG."

"THIS IS A MYSTERIOUS CASE," HE SAID.

"THE LITTLE GIRL'S MOTHER TOOK HER HOME, AND PUT HER TO BED... HER HEAD THROBBED."

"HER LITTLE BROTHER CAME IN, AND SAID, 'MAYBE YOUR EARS ARE TOO TIGHT.'"

SO HE LOOSENED EACH EAR ONE TURN BACK. HER HEADACHE SUDDENLY STOPPED, AND SHE NEVER HAD ANOTHER HEADACHE AGAIN.

I GUESS HE DIDN'T LIKE IT.... THAT WAS HIS "GOOD LUCK, YOU'RE GOING TO NEED IT" HANDSHAKE!

WHAT IN THE WORLD ARE YOU DOING?

ONE MINUTE YOU'RE IN CENTER FIELD, AND THE NEXT MINUTE YOU'RE GONE! WHAT KIND OF BALL PLAYER ARE YOU?!!

I WAS STANDING OUT THERE IN CENTER FIELD, CHARLIE BROWN, AND I WAS PAYING ATTENTION LIKE YOU ALWAYS TELL ME TO DO...

SUDDENLY, OUT OF NOWHERE, I HEARD A PIECE OF CAKE CALLING ME!

TEETH MARKS

HAVE YOU BEEN CHEWING ON MY NEW BAT?!!

WHAT SORT OF A STUPID DOG ARE YOU? DON'T YOU HAVE ANY MORE SENSE THAN TO CHEW ON A BASEBALL BAT?!

IF YOU HAVE TO CHEW ON SOMETHING, CAN'T YOU FIND A STICK OR A BONE OR A FENCE OR SOMETHING? DO YOU HAVE TO RUIN A GOOD BASEBALL BAT?! WHY CAN'T YOU...

HE DIDN'T CHEW ON YOUR BAT..I USED IT TO HIT ROCKS!

DO YOU WANT A BITE?

SCHULZ

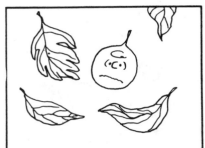

I HATE IT WHEN THE BASEBALL SEASON IS OVER

THERE'S A DREARINESS IN THE AIR THAT DEPRESSES ME...

EVERYTHING SEEMS SAD...EVEN THE OL' PITCHER'S MOUND IS COVERED WITH WEEDS...

I GUESS ALL A PERSON CAN DO IS DREAM HIS DREAMS...MAYBE I'LL BE A GOOD BALL PLAYER SOMEDAY...MAYBE I'LL EVEN PLAY IN THE WORLD SERIES, AND BE A HERO...

I BET I WILL PLAY IN THE WORLD SERIES SOMEDAY...I BET I'LL...

HEY! LOOK WHO'S OUT HERE TALKING TO HIMSELF!

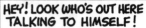

WHAT ARE YOU DOING, CHARLIE BROWN, THINKING ABOUT ALL THE TIMES YOU STRUCK OUT?!

THERE'S A DREARINESS IN THE AIR THAT DEPRESSES ME!

HERE, CATCH!

OW! MY HEAD!

AAUGH! I'M BLEEDING!

I'M BLEEDING TO DEATH! I'M BLEEDING TO DEATH!

SOMEBODY HELP ME! I'M BLEEDING TO DEATH! I'M BLEEDING TO DEATH!

OH, CUT IT OUT! IT WAS JUST A RUBBER BALL..

IT WAS?

I'VE NEVER KNOWN ANYONE WHO COULD GET SO EXCITED OVER NOTHING!

I WANT TO APOLOGIZE FOR MAKING SUCH A SCENE, CHARLIE BROWN...

I THOUGHT MY LIFE'S BLOOD WAS DRAINING AWAY!

HERE'S THE FIERCE MOUNTAIN LION WAITING FOR HIS VICTIM...

AUGH!

SOMEHOW MY ATTACKS ALWAYS SEEM TO LACK FORCE!

THIS IS NATIONAL DOG WEEK

THIS IS NATIONAL DOG WEEK

CONGRATULATIONS!

I WANT YOU TO KNOW THAT I'M BEHIND YOU ONE-HUNDRED PERCENT!

DOG WEEK

I THINK IT'S WONDERFUL WHEN A PERSON LIKE YOURSELF TAKES THE TIME TO PROMOTE SUCH A REALLY WORTH-WHILE CAUSE...

NATIONAL DOG WEEK

GOOD LUCK TO YOU AND YOUR ORGANIZATION

THAT SORT OF THING ALWAYS EMBARRASSES ME!

SCHULZ

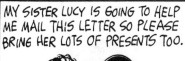

I SUPPOSE YOU'RE ALL WONDERING WHY I'VE ASKED YOU HERE TODAY...

IF YOU THROW THAT SNOWBALL AT ME, I'LL HAVE THE HUMANE SOCIETY ON YOU SO FAST IT'LL MAKE YOUR HEAD SWIM!

WHOEVER PAINTS THOSE SIGNS FOR HIM, DOES A GOOD JOB!

SAY! I LIKE THAT CAP, LUCY!

THANK YOU..

YOU'RE ALL SET FOR COLD WEATHER, AREN'T YOU?

YES, I GUESS I AM..

YOU KNOW WHAT IT'S LIKE TO BE COLD AND UNCOMFORTABLE, DON'T YOU?

OH, YES...I KNOW THAT FEELING...

YOU LIKE ANIMALS, DON'T YOU? I MEAN, YOU'VE ALWAYS BEEN SORT OF AN ANIMAL LOVER, HAVEN'T YOU?

OF COURSE!

DOGS, TOO? ESPECIALLY DOGS WHO SLEEP OUTSIDE, AND SHIVER AND SHAKE ALL NIGHT?

SIGH

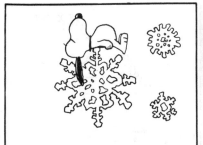

Happiness is catching snowflakes on your tongue.

SCHULZ

Happiness is a Christmas vacation with no book reports to write.

DEAR SANTA CLAUS, HOW HAVE YOU BEEN?

PLEASE DON'T GET THE IDEA THAT I AM WRITING BECAUSE I WANT SOMETHING.

NOTHING COULD BE FURTHER FROM THE TRUTH. I WANT NOTHING.

IF YOU WANT TO SKIP OUR HOUSE THIS YEAR, GO RIGHT AHEAD. I WON'T BE OFFENDED. REALLY I WON'T.

SPEND YOUR TIME ELSEWHERE. DON'T BOTHER WITH ME. I REALLY MEAN IT.

WHAT IN THE WORLD KIND OF LETTER IS THIS?!!

I'M HOPING THAT HE'LL FIND MY ATTITUDE PECULIARLY REFRESHING

SCHULZ